SUCCESS IN CELIBACY

by

SHEA SCOTT EDWARDS

PUBLISHED BY BLUE ARTISTS, LLC

I first and foremost dedicate this book to the Holy Spirit for giving me the supernatural ability to fight the good fight of faith. To my seventeen-year-old self, to the late Shari Mack for taking the time to instill the principle of the "Season of Stillness", to my loving father for affirming me as a writer, and to my darling husband Brandon for being my partner in purpose and walking the unpopular path with me, I dedicate this book to you.

CONTENTS

SUCCESS IN CELIBACY

INTRODUCTION

I get it - you only live once, right? Why would anyone opt to sacrifice the lust and allure of orgasmic elation today for a tomorrow which isn't even promised? Millennials are programmed to believe life is all about seizing the moment and capturing it in the most coveted selfie. As an educated artist and progressive thinker, I spent years questioning whether to answer the call to exchange my sexual freedom for the sake of experiencing real intimacy with God. After all, is it really that serious?

Although I was eventually able to be celibate for six years, it took many attempts at slipping and falling (clears throat) in and out of bed and self-medicating my guilt, before I could consistently abstain from premarital sex. After one too many nauseating morning afters, putting back on the panties from the night before and taking the covert walk of shame, I realized by engaging in premarital sex I was in way over my head. Sin was creating a lasting imprint that gargling Listerine and taking hot showers couldn't fix. By making the choice to live young, wild and free, I was ultimately doing myself a disservice. The following scripture began to resonate:

Flee from sexual immorality. All other sins a person commits are outside the body, but whoever sins sexually, sins against their own body.
1 Corinthians 6:18

We all pick our poisons. Yet, out of all the debauchery one can partake, why does the Bible deem premarital sex as the only sin committed against oneself? The answer is simple. By having sex outside of marriage, we are subjecting ourselves to personal pain (covertly disguised as gain) and what's worse... separation from God. Many are not aware that they are willfully harming themselves in the pursuit of personal pleasure. Think of it this way; sex, like eating processed food and sweets tastes so good in the moment. Yet, overtime, its indulgence quietly causes internal disease. On the other hand, celibacy, like eating vegetables, is a vital part of cultivating a healthy, spiritual lifestyle. Without it, we'll never wholeheartedly experience spiritual empowerment and peace. By prematurely connecting our spirits to another, we are forfeiting the countless benefits that come along with an intimate, personal relationship with Christ. In other words, the only way to truly please yourself is to first please God.

When we make the commitment to sacrifice temporary pleasure for the sake of honoring God, we are setting ourselves up to see the promises of God fully come to pass in our lives. If you, like I once was, are still grappling with the notion of celibacy, I'd bet you can relate to wanting to be successful. Like a pent-up fire yearning to set the world a flame, we are hungry to realize our dreams and live up to our greatest potential. What if I told you the key to your success in life lies in your obedience to God?

You are God's chosen instrument. According to your purity shall be your success. It is not grot great talent; it is not great ideas that God uses; it is great likeness to Jesus Christ.
-Robert Murray McCheyne

Success in any area of life begins by making one simple decision. It is never too late; you are never too old or broken to begin anew, to take one step in the direction that will forever change the trajectory of your life and eternal existence.

Each person has a unique reason for deciding to either stop having premarital sex or to maintain one's virginity until marriage. Success in celibacy becomes inevitable to the one who upholds the position that giving in is simply not an option. As my dad always says, "A winner never quits and a quitter never wins". A life of abstinence can be an insurmountable feat to any human being operating out of their own strength. Yet the Bible says, "I can do all things through Christ who strengthens me". What then about celibacy is any different? Allow the fact that you've chosen to read this book serve as confirmation that God not only has thoughts about you in this intimate area of your life, but wants to empower you to be successful and kept Holy unto Himslef in order to carry out your Divine purpose.

I'd like to begin by debunking the notion of becoming celibate, maintaining a vow of abstinence or wearing the never coveted badge of "born-again" virgin. While sex is the one thing we've been programmed by society to believe we can't nor shouldn't live without, once we've truly surrendered our bodies to be used as instruments of the Holy Spirit, we are divinely equipped to become more than conquerors over our flesh. Allow the Holy Spirit to serve as your guide and greatest ally in moments of uncertainty and weakness along this supernatural adventure.

The world will argue celibacy is an archaic practice only deemed socially acceptable when done willingly or as a bi-product of new age enlightenment. The enemy has distorted and devalued the divine purpose of sex so much that even those of us who desire to live a life that is pleasing to our Creator feel demonized for taking such a stand for righteousness' sake.

In recent years, a few celebrities, who are at best viewed as being willfully radical to the mainstream media, have opened about their celibate journeys. The rest of us, men in particular, do not acquire the badge of being brave and noble and are often placed in one of two categories: idealistic extremists or sexually repressed Jesus freaks. All in all, it's much easier to buy into the lies about sex than to stand in the truth and remain pure until the designated season.

Celibacy is a journey that requires the proper requisites to guarantee success. It is a conflict between the spirit and flesh. Once we've been transformed by the renewing of our minds, we're then empowered to make our mind/body obey the Holy Spirit dwelling within. Once I changed my mindset and accepted the Bible as the standard of truth in my life, I was given supernatural courage, discernment, determination and discipline. God will do the same for you if you trust and believe.

The first step towards becoming successful in celibacy is to believe with your whole heart God has and wants more for you. Next, you must dare to step out of the natural by exchanging your carnal mindset for the new mind of Christ.

Therefore, if anyone is in Christ, the new creation has come:
The old has gone, the new is here!
2 Corinthians 5:7

Whether you're currently engaging in casual sex, abstinate by choice or chance, in a relationship or engaged to be married—simply resolve in your mind to make the choice to honor God by embarking upon the celibate journey. Be determined to be more than a conqueror in this area of your life. Trust the Holy Spirit to guide you to the finish line. After all, you're not saying no to sex forever, just for now. Remember, celibacy is a temporary season!

This book is about allowing God to take His rightful place as Lord of your life while providing practical tools to help simplify your actions in obedience to His Will, *which is the highest good for your life.* Each chapter represents a fundamental principle I had to master in order to break free from (the dirty word) fornication and a distorted since of self-worth. While there's no secret formula to obeying God, my hope is that my transparent journey of trial and error will help dissuade you from unnecessary pitfalls along this sacred road. No matter what season of life you are in, I'm a living witness that you can be successful in celibacy. It's time for you to break free and stay free from living beneath God's best! By faith, declare your success in this area of your life, for you have already overcome.

Ye are of God, little children, and have overcome them: because greater is he that is in you, than he that is in the world.
1 John 4:4

My Journey

Let's talk about you and me
Let's talk about all the good things
And the bad things that may be
Let's talk about sex … -Salt & Pepper

It's common knowledge the church advocates single people to abstain from having sex. Yet from my observation they rarely succeed at communicating, from a place of love, why and how celibacy is an essential practice in the life of a believer. Is it because many of our parents, pastors, clergy were not successful themselves and lack the wisdom to guide us down the sacred road of abstinence from a place of experience? If we are going to be a triumphant generation and prepare the world for the return of Christ, we must remove the stigma that comes with talking about sex in our churches and communities. The time has come for us to be transparent about our struggles by allowing God's truth to shine a light on the darkness and distorted messages we as millennials are flooded with daily. Join me in an authentic dialogue about sex and sexuality.

Everyone can relate to having an innate curiosity about sexuality. For me, it began even before puberty. My mom had a secret book stashed away on how to tell your child about the birds and the bees, in stages. I'd first read about female parts and the ins and outs of menstruation. Fascinated with the human anatomy, I'd skip ahead and read about male parts and then sex and sexuality. I learned early how our bodies are intrinsically designed to function as sexual beings.

Although reserved in nature, I was confident existing in my own skin yet always eager to grow to the next stage of development and for the freedom to take on womanly wings. As strange as it sounds, I couldn't wait to start growing hair under my arm pits, as it was an unspoken sign of going from little girl to, well....older girl. Always eager for the next stage of growing up, I prayed to God for big breasts and to receive my menstrual cycle as soon as my older cousin got hers.

The images I saw from an early age directly impacted my view on sex and sexuality. When I was a young girl, my granny allowed me to watch "The Young and the Restless" with her. Images of passionate love making began to subliminally normalize and glamorize sex outside the context of marriage.

As a pre-teen, my best friend and I would sit in her bedroom plotting our first kiss with our boy crushes. My mind was set on kissing the boy with gold braces who'd later become my high school sweetheart. Sure enough, when time and opportunity presented itself, driven by a force of raging hormones, I found myself hiding behind a red barn-like shed kissing lips that tasted like cherry Chap Stick. What can I say; I had a thing for pretty boys? I'll never forget my first kiss; it was exhilarating, adventurous and romantic (as puppy love can be).

After the thrill quickly fizzled out, the butterflies I'd experienced earlier that day had turned into a queasy feeling in the pit of my belly. I was experiencing my first taste of conviction. Although my flesh was gratified and I'd finally had a real kiss, something in my gut didn't feel right. I felt like I had something to hide. It was time to go home to face up with my folks, just not quite as innocent as they'd previously known me. Sitting at the dinner table that night, my appetite was gone and I picked up my dinner fork with a shaky, sweaty palm. I was barely able to look my father in the eye. Although I was in the eighth grade, and innocent compared to most girls my age, what was this guilt I was feeling? Sneaking around was supposed to be a normal teenage rite of passage. I felt deep down inside, my father across the table knew and I had somehow disappointed him. The layers of innocence I was once eager to peel away left me feeling more naked and vulnerable than expected.

Brought up in church, I was no stranger to God. At age seven, I felt the gentle nudging of the Holy Spirit. I courageously walked down the aisle at church to give my life to Christ. From that moment on, I was proud to accept my place in the Kingdom as a child of God. After losing my brother in middle school, I can honestly say I was very clear about my faith, and what it meant to walk with the Lord. In my darkest youthful hour, I could feel the presence of The Holy Spirit hovering about to comfort me. The Lord would steady my heart and illuminate scripture. I found great solace reading passages from the book of Psalms. My relationship with God was distinct and personal. I knew Him to be a friend and experienced the supernatural power of God turning my sorrow into joy. His strength kept a smile on my face and joy in my heart. I learned at an early age to trust in the plans of God amid loss and confusion. I was centered in the hope that I would one day experience eternal life and reunite with my brother again.

When high school hit, I should have been more concerned with finding my identity in Christ than emulating the steps of others. A select few girls who I considered to be pretty and popular had already volunteered their virginity. While I enjoyed the occasional make-out session, that was as far as I was willing to go. My priorities were in order (or so I thought). I was focused on following in the footsteps of my older, beautiful, athletic, popular cousins. Making the cheerleading squad, getting good grades, being on homecoming court and making my parents proud were on the forefront of my brain. However, I did wonder if the heat would turn up in terms of pressure from high school boys to go further than my backyard, barn yard kiss.

Ninth grade was a good year for me. Classes were a breeze. I made the cheerleading squad and I was selected to be on homecoming court as I'd dreamed. However, Homecoming, like prom, left much to be conquered by the teenaged boy privileged enough to attend in the ninth grade. Because of my stance on remaining a virgin, I was dumped on two occasions.

Word got around my high school that the cheerful, naïve ample-bosomed cheerleader wasn't giving it up or giving in. When tenth grade came around, my first kiss companion became my boyfriend. Moreover, my confidence was way up. We were highly coveted high school sweethearts, if I must say, and I'd beat out the girls who'd given it up. The coat tails of his virginity were long gone and still, for some reason, he wanted me. Perhaps he felt I was worth the challenge more so than the wait.

I got by for two years without giving in. My fear of teen pregnancy and not wanting to disgrace my family coupled with conviction from the Holy Spirit kept me steadfast. I remember going on church retreats with other teenagers my age. By this time, having sex was commonplace even amongst the church community. Everyone was exploring and seemingly having a good time. While my boyfriend and I began having more and more intimate encounters, my conviction still outweighed my curiosity.

At age 17, I reached a spiritual crossroad. I'd made it through middle school with flying colors and was on my way to making it out of high school with my v-card. At this point, we'd done just about everything but go all the way, so what was I waiting for? My inner voice, that quiet knowing, kept nudging me to just wait until marriage. But marriage seemed a long time away. I knew my boyfriend wouldn't wait forever and I wasn't willing to lose my relationship. He hung with a group of older, privileged suburban "play" boys who encouraged him to "pull and smash" as many girls as possible.

Amidst the rumors of him cheating, my teenage heart couldn't fathom such betrayal. He preyed on my naiveté and told me what I needed to hear to feel secure. The threat of losing him made me cling on even tighter. After all, we'd spent so much time together, so when did he have time to cheat? When we were together, I was his priority.

As time went on, I began feeling more and more pressure to give in; after all, I'd been with the same guy (first kiss) for going on two years and he was patient enough to wait despite all the other girls who wanted him. I later found out he had no trouble waiting because he wasn't truly waiting. Like a wolf in sheep's clothing, he was having sex behind my back. He was celebrated for being a player while everyone was snickering about my stupidity on the sidelines.

Then life through a huge curve ball. My mother became very ill. Her illness took away a portion of the parental safeguard keeping me at home on weekend nights. She was physically present but mentally aloof. The carpet had been pulled from underneath me. My stable home life was shaken to its core. Very few people knew what I was going through. I was scared and clamoring to cling to the familiar. I prayed to God for my mother's healing, but He wasn't answering my prayers quickly enough. Trials are an invitation for us to draw closer to Christ. Yet, I went in the opposite direction and allowed my pain to distract me from my convictions about remaining a virgin.

My boyfriend became my greatest emotional support system. I became infatuated with the scent of his Polo cologne, tight hugs and soft lips. He always knew just what to say and how to say it. Not a day went by without him calling me beautiful.

He was a shoulder to cry on and would sweep me away in his fancy, red Rodeo truck. With the fresh Virginia wind blowing in my face, the base of his obnoxiously loud sound system drowned out the noise of my fear. He showered me with expensive gifts and helped me live out many a teen age fantasy date night.

Also around this time, I'd been selected to join the cast of a popular show on BET which was casting out of

Washington, DC. They were looking for teenagers with strong opinions about urban issues. Being on this show was a dream come true for me. In front of the camera, I was an advocate for teens waiting until marriage. My co-stars treated me like a doe-eyed young girl. Still, the Holy Spirit told me I was special to God and He desired for me to remain a virgin. In a society where sex sells and "everyone is doing it", the heat was on. I was one of the few still standing. Behind closed doors, I continued praying for my mom and questioning my gut. I was on the brink of giving it up to the cheater I was in love with.

In hindsight, I wish I had someone to iterate I didn't have to say NO forever; I just should've said wait. I was looking for someone or some message to encourage me, in love, to listen to His voice and remain pure-to remind me of my worth and of the cost that was paid by my Savior. While I inherently knew my mom was not encouraging me to have sex, she supported me going on birth control, "just in case something happened". While it was indeed wise to make a concerted effort to avoid teenage pregnancy, the act of sex should never be a "just in case" occurrence. Yet, I was 17 now. My mother was confident in the foundation of strong spiritual values she'd instilled in me. The time had come for me to hold myself accountable to the personal relationship I had with God.

My high school sweetheart was tenacious in getting his way by asking the age old question, "Can I please just put the head in?" I allowed him to poke me a time or two before going all the way. Each time, I stopped him because like that of most virgins, my body was rejecting his entrance. My spirit wasn't ready.

One afternoon, we were hanging out in his bedroom and I decided to surrender my virginity. I was expecting there to be some pain, and there was. The feeling of penetration was not pleasurable and remained painful for quite some time. I'd now compromised and couldn't even enjoy it. I initially felt the same guilt I felt when I could barely look my father in the eye at the dinner table. This time, I could barely look my spiritual father (GOD) in the eye. Sin had created a major crack in our relationship.

In hindsight, I wonder why I didn't just stop after that initial time. Once I gave away my virginity, I sort of felt like there was no turning back. Most of my peers were no longer virgins so I might as well remain in the club. A cunning trick of the enemy is to distance us from our conviction. God is always waiting with open arms for us to repent, change our behavior and turn back to Him.

Then came college. Over time, that nauseating conviction became drowned out by more freedom, more boys, college experimentation, greater sexual feats, and more obligatory feelings of giving it up in a relationship.

Going from being a small-town girl from Richmond, V.A. to living in Washington, D.C., I was exposed to so many things. I played it relatively safe the first one to two years of college either in a serious relationship, or just messing around with one or two college boys. By my junior year, clubbing became the norm, smoking weed was a ritual and I worked as a waitress in sports clubs and upscale lounges for extra cash. Having sex, being sensual and comfortable in one's sexuality appeared to be the next rite of passage as an educated, independent young woman.

After my next serious relationship ended with a charming Howard young man, bred in the upper echelon of society, I was left with a very bruised ego. I had to find a way to regain my power. I got the bright idea to experiment, push my limits and regain my power by having a one-night stand.

I came across many young professionals and attractive suitors at the sports bar where I worked. I felt so liberated by the idea of hand picking the guy lucky enough to have a one night stand with me. I chose a guy whom I'd seen come in from time to time. In the dim lighting, he was tall and muscular with an air of mystery —the perfect candidate to scratch the itch of my curiosity. What would it feel like to be with someone purely for sex? I was finally in control. I wasn't doing it out of guilt or obligation. I was doing it merely on the quest to find liberation. As conscious as I thought I was, I was blind to the fact I was literally entering the devil's domain.

He entered my apartment in the dark. He left in the dark. Thank God I had sense enough to make him use protection. The next day, no call, no text. The feeling of liberation and power I was seeking quickly dissipated into a bottomless pit of emptiness. My ego was further bruised and self-esteem quietly damaged. Although I initiated the act, I felt used. The worst part was I'd devalued myself and felt the ill effects of turning to a man for comfort instead of turning to my Heavenly Father who was grieved by such acts.

About three days later he called and gave some random excuse as to why he had to abruptly leave. He continued to reach out to reconvene for quite a while, but it only took one time for me to learn that one night stands weren't for me. A small part of me left with him in the dark that night. An even larger part of my relationship with God was compromised. The only time I attended church in all four years of my undergraduate career was when I visited home. While still present, the voice of the Holy Spirit was getting drowned out by the enemy's lie that I was in control of my own body and was free to do with it whatever I pleased.

While I prayed for forgiveness and protection, God was jealous for my affection. Shunned by the world, the notion of being a "born again virgin" or turning over a new leaf of abstinence seemed inauthentic. The standard set by my Heavenly Father to remain pure seemed further and further out of my grasp.

Do not worship any other god, for the LORD, whose name is Jealous, is a jealous God. **Exodus 34:14**

I moved to Los Angeles immediately following undergradate school and boy did I unleash my inner hippie. I was mesmerized by the sense of freedom and a "no worries" attitude California natives exuded. I was introduced to the "city of angels" by a family friend and successful film editor. He took me on one of my first nights on the town to a roof top, wrap party. People were smoking weed in public. I'd reached the promised land! I submerged myself in love of the arts, sensual exploration and marijuana while my disobedience transitioned to a whole new level. As an aspiring actress, far away from the lingering cares of home, I was blinded by the flashing lights and the fantasy of making it to the big screen. I even began to question if Jesus was the only way to get to God. The enemy will use fun and a false sense of freedom to lure you further and further into the dark. It's amazing how deep I was walking in darkness in a city with so much sun.

I dated often and tested the limits of my sexual boundaries with an array of young men. Only having sex with a select few, I was searching for something deeper. I had my fun, but was never fully fulfilled. My spiritual well was running dry. Every time I engaged in sex outside of marriage, I felt empty.

LA was where I had a re-awakening of my relationship with God. Jesus was calling me closer and there was no longer any time to run or straddle the fence.

If I were to acknowledge my being a daughter of the most high God, I had to change my behavior and walk according to His ways. The Lord wanted me for Himself. To be honest, I was tired of feeling depressed after every sexual encounter, tired of seeking the spiritual from the physical, feeling empty, used, overlooked and disobedient. It was time for me stop having sex. I needed to repent and turn back to my initial conviction to wait until marriage. As such a heavy conviction, I could only bear it by staying at the Father's feet.

Don't be surprised when such a declaration is made; the enemy will send the best of the best to tempt you out of your vow to God. An old friend from high school, now professional athlete, had moved to town. We'd always had a quiet spark, but when I saw him after all those years there was a magnetic pull of attraction. I had plans of being celibate, but this one I could NOT resist. While it ended up being a sexually gratifying experience, it was just that, sex—no love, no relationship, no friendship, just sex. Driven by pure lust, he'd call and I'd come. On the drives back home at night, there I was again just me and God. I was broken and God was patiently waiting for me to remain in His sacred arms to cry and to heal, to strengthen me enough to wait. He had so much more in store.

Fast forward to when I heard the words, "You don't just fall into bed with someone; you make the decision", a light switch went off. These simple words, given by a trusted spiritual mentor, empowered me at a most critical time along the last leg of my celibate journey. From this moment on, I knew I forever held the power in overcoming temptation. If I were to have sex before marriage, I could no longer blame it on getting lost in the moment. It would be because I consciously chose to do so. It was apparent that my love for God had ascended to a place where willful disobedience could no longer stand.

The spell was broken and I now stood atop shattered broken pieces of the dirty word, fornication, confident I'd complete my race with power and success. The chains of being a voluntary participant of pre-marital sex were permanently broken.

Do you not know that your bodies are temples of the Holy Spirit, who is in you, whom you have received from God? You are not your own; you were bought at a price. Therefore honor God with your bodies.
1 Corinthians 19:20 NIV

LOVE

And you shall love the Lord your God with all your heart,
with all your soul, with all your mind, and with all your
strength. This is the first commandment.

Mark 12:30

Most people can relate to either loving the idea of being in love or loving the feeling of sex. Trouble is we are too willing to compromise our spiritual compass to obtain such "love". The pursuit of lust over-complicates things. Whether it is a person, a goal or a material possession, we'll do whatever it takes to get what we want. The question is: are we willing to demonstrate our love for God by pursing a relationship with Him with the same tenacity and fervor?

When we first fall madly in love with Christ, taking in the all-encompassing depth of how much He first loved us, we are empowered, through love, (not guilt, fear, or condemnation) to remain obedient. When we love, and revere our Heavenly Father, being in a right relationship becomes our priority. A genuine LOVE for God is the only way to not feel trivial or fearful about maintaining a celibate lifestyle.

For God so loved the world that he gave his one and only Son, that whoever believes in him shall not perish but have eternal life. For God did not send his Son into the world to condemn the world, but to save the world through him.

John 3:16-17

After various failed attempts of falling and having to pick up my broken pieces, I grew tired of feeling depressed and convicted. If I was going to be successful at being celibate, I knew I had to get serious about my relationship with God. The shame that came along with willingly falling short of the standard I knew God was calling me to live up to became too hard a burden to bear. I could no longer ignore the voice of the Lord and his steadfast pursuit of my attention and devotion. He wanted me to value myself in the same way He valued me. I can't tell you the countless times my heart would break knowing I was breaking the heart of my first love Jesus. Still, while conviction prompted my decision to get serious about the celibate journey, it was only my love for God that saw me through to the end.

If ye love me, keep my commandments. **John 14:15-31**

Take a moment to consider your relationship with God. By considering your relationship I don't mean tracking the number of Sundays you go to church. Think about your relationship with God as if no one else existed, just you and your Creator. Take a moment to bring the great love He has for you to the forefront of your consciousness. Have you accepted the fact that Jesus is madly in love with you? It was out of the eternal love of God the Father that you were created.

For you created my inmost being; you knit me together in my mother's womb.
I praise you because I am fearfully and wonderfully made; your works are wonderful, I know that full well. My frame was not hidden from you when I was made in the secret place, when I was woven together in the depths of the earth.
Psalm 139:13-15

God loved you so much, He gave His only son Jesus Christ, His most prized possession (free of sin), to die on the cross to save you from having to pay the penalty of every sin (He already knew you would commit), knowing you are incapable of perfection.

God doesn't desire you to wait to have sex until marriage to punish, but to have you bask in the loving union He pre-destined you to have, first with Him, free from the burden of sin. Having an awareness of even a small portion of the love God has for you should be a compelling enough reason to put His Will before your own. Many of us continue to fall because we haven't taken on the weight of the depth of His unconditional love for us. God loves us through our sins and in spite of them.

Where can I go from your Spirit? Where can I flee from your presence? If I go up to the heavens, you are there; if I make my bed in the depths, you are there.
Psalm 139:7-8

You may be wondering if Jesus has already paid for my sins, why can't you just continue living the way you want and ask for forgiveness later, since the grace of God will always forgive you anyway? After all, there are way worse things one can do than to have sex before marriage. If I relate this question to a normal relationship with a cheating partner, it's impossible to continue hurting someone you truly love. On a basic level, at some point your actions need to line up with your words if you are serious about doing your part to uphold a lasting relationship. The same goes for our relationship with God. Once we've accepted His love for us and fallen madly in love with Him, that love causes us to rise up to a higher standard of action to honor the love.

In addition, once we accept Christ as our personal Lord and Savior, we are no longer prisoners to sin. Once you begin walking in the truth of your spiritual transformation though Christ, you must begin making steps towards dying to the old way of living.

What shall we say then? Shall we continue in sin, that grace may abound? God forbid. How shall we, that are dead to sin, live any longer therein?
Romans 6:1-3

Do yourself a favor and elect to embark upon the celibate journey out of a love for God, not self-gain. Yes, God has promises for your future. It's natural to want to be married while trusting God to send your spouse. However, as a word of caution: do not allow your love for God to be based on conditions, timelines or personal aspirations. True love has nothing to do with what you hope to benefit. Pure love stands on its own. Jesus has already paid the price for you to live in a relationship with Him. I encourage you to love God for who He is, not for who or what you want Him to provide.

Still set on making it as an actress in Hollywood, I admit I've tried bargaining with the Lord in hopes that my obedience would move Him to bless my career in the way and time I envisioned. Remember, God is the potter and we are the clay. He sets the rules in which we are free to obey. There's a finite difference. We cannot earn our righteousness or manipulate our way into being blessed.

As time goes on, your true motives will surface. Don't convolute your celibate walk by doing it for self-gain. You are free to remove personal ambition out of the equation when it comes to your love for God. He doesn't need it. Your steps have already been ordered. Your husband or wife has already been pre-ordained. Now is the time to simply bask in your love for God. Allow this love to be enough.

While God wants us to fear and revere Him, love is more powerful than fear! Living for God out of a place of fear of being damned to hell will be an agonizing walk. The celibate journey eventually becomes effortless when you do it out of a love for God in pursuit of earthly peace and eternal life.

Until we allow ourselves to fully experience the unconditional, eternal love that Christ has for us, we can never be faithful to God (much less love ourselves or anyone else). Success in celibacy becomes inescapable once we've shifted our priorities. We are to first and foremost love God with all our heart, mind and soul. The Bible teaches us that if we love God, we will obey Him. It's as simple as that.

Pray this prayer with me:

Father God, we come humbly before you declaring that you are indeed the true and living God our Father. We come seeking your love in a way that we've never experienced before. Let your unconditional love cover our hurts, fears, doubts, insecurities and desires. We are grateful for your grace and mercy that covers a multitude of sin. We commit our relationship to you because we know you loved us first and you are worthy of our affection. Show us your love in a way that will forever inspire us to live in obedience to your will.

OBEDIENCE

Living a life in obedience to God is my greatest ambition and will one day become my greatest accomplishment.
–Minister Ronald Weekly

Daring to obey God is a gamble that you're sure to win. While we may have many ambitions in life, obedience to God must become our number one priority. Once we maintain the position that our purpose in this life is to cultivate a walk, in harmony with God's will, we will achieve success in every area of life, including celibacy.

Victory did not come because of personal will alone. Breaking old habits, changing patterns of thinking, and sticking to one's decisions is not an easy task, but with God's help, very possible. While fear of failure may be present, know this: when obedience to God becomes your greatest priority, heaven is in your corner. Once you make the decision, know that He has empowered you to carry it out to the very end.

The hard part: Now that we've made up in our minds to embark upon the celibate journey, we are no longer free to justify disobedience. In other words, when you know better you must do better. When we opt to gratify our flesh, we must be man/woman enough to own up to our iniquity. Ouch! Harsh word, I know. However, no matter where we are, being transparent before the Lord will set us free.

The good news: Once we've been saved by grace we are no longer held captive to sin! Our spirit is more powerful than our flesh and he whom the Son sets free, is free indeed. The next step is to align our decisions according to the Will of God.

What good is it for someone to gain the whole world, yet forfeit their soul?
Mark 8:36

God wants us to live empowered lives without anything standing in the way of our relationship with Him and the fulfillment of our destiny. Engaging in sex outside of God's intended purpose distorts our vision. It causes us to walk through life with cloudy vision, making it more and more difficult to unmistakably hear from God. Distorted vision can even cause us to get stuck in unhealthy soul ties with individuals with whom God never intended us to attach.

The Bible teaches us that obedience is better than sacrifice. It's better to preserve our virginity than to have sex and later make the decision to become celibate. Better, not because we are in any way able to "earn" our righteousness yet, because maintaining a position of obedience saves days, weeks, and years of having to peel away and heal from the layers of disobedience to God. If you, like me, gave up your virginity too soon, the blood of Jesus has the power to cleanse every stain. Rededicating your body to God redeems the time and gives your mind, body, and soul the time needed to properly heal.

Once we've opened the door to sin, choosing to abstain from sex before marriage may feel like a tremendous sacrifice. The Bible says the presentation of our bodies as a living sacrifice is our reasonable service. While God is pleased when we do so, He considers it our reasonable service. The sacrifice of celibacy is our true and proper worship. It is wonderful to worship God amongst other believers on Sunday morning. Yet, have you ever considered your celibate walk an act of worship?

Do not offer any part of yourself to sin as an instrument of wickedness, but rather offer yourselves to God as those who have been brought from death to life; and offer every part of yourself to him as an instrument of righteousness.

Romans 6:13

You were created by God for the purpose of God.
–Pastor Rick Warren

He longs to entrust us with vision and purpose. However, we do ourselves a disservice by not remaining in the optimal place of receptivity which comes from a life of obedient surrender. The power of celibacy enables us to have a clear head to hear from God about His purpose for our lives and later see our mate for who they really are.

Once I pursued obedience with reckless abandon, I received the freedom that came from complete surrender. Fully commit to picking up your cross to follow Him down the road less traveled path of righteousness where limitations cease to exist. Surrender to the fact that there is no turning back. Although you cannot see it now, where God is taking you is more fulfilling than where you've been.

If your reason for having sex is to gratify yourself or please another person, it is better to please God than to please man. The truth is, the only way to find true fulfillment is to first, please God. No matter how long or committed the relationship, by having premarital sex, we step out of alignment with God's perfect will. The small, still voice of conviction will never allow us to have genuine peace. Living a surrendered life in obedience to God is the only way to find true peace and fulfillment.

No one can serve two masters. Either you will hate the one and love the other, or you will be devoted to the one and despise the other.
Matthew 6:24

Peace is the foundation for spiritual receptivity and self-empowerment. Whether we choose to acknowledge it or not, there is a feeling of shame that comes with having sex outside of marriage. The Bible illustrates this clearly in the Garden of Eden with the shame Adam and Eve felt after disobeying God when they sought to hide and cover themselves. Jesus died on the cross to set us free from guilt and shame. However, to obtain this freedom, we must gain the courage to walk in obedience. When we replace our desire to gratify our flesh with a commitment to our purpose, there isn't anything we cannot achieve.

Know your worth! Before testing your ability to delve into the deep waters of celibacy, understand your value. God has already created and handpicked you to answer this call. Know that you have been chosen to walk in obedience and remain pure. This is your reasonable service. Anyone can carry out religious practices on Sunday. We are challenged to worship the Lord with our mind, body and soul. After all, He wants it all because He owns it all.

The Lord has chosen you to be his treasured possession.
Deut. 14:2

Pray this prayer with me:

Dear Lord, I pray that you give me power over anything hindering my ability to remain obedient to you. I admit I often neglect to try abstaining from sex due to my fear of failure and disappointing you. I lack confidence in my ability to maintain self-control. There have been times when I've given into the lie that I can't live without sex. Dear Lord, I ask that you fill me so much with your presence and love that it overpowers my need for affection, attention, and physical gratification until the designated Season. It is my desire to be obedient to your Will. By faith, I thank you in advance for giving me the strength remain pure in your sight and for the new level of intimacy I will find in my relationship with you.

SEASON OF STILLNESS

Now that you're fully intrigued by the notion of celibacy, this is the perfect time to self-reflect. Begin with an intentional self-analysis. What are your personal strengths, weakness, fears and blocks towards maintaining a celibate lifestyle? Highlight areas needing improvement —the good, the bad and the ugly. Be 100% honest with yourself about the love you show yourself because this directly informs the decisions you make. Identify the people in your life helping or hindering you from heading in the direction of your best self.

Before God can entrust you with your mate, He wants you to love yourself fully and wholly. Do you enjoy your own company? Yes, you may have a "type" and know what you are attracted to, but what do you like/love about yourself? Make a list of your top 10 qualities and strengths. Bring awareness to your daily internal dialogue. It is a direct reflection of your self-esteem and how you feel God thinks about you. What are some of the thoughts you think about yourself? How do your thoughts align with the thoughts God has for you? Do you feel worthy of being loved, honored and respected? Do you feel you are worth the wait? Put it all on the table and learn to be transparent with yourself in the presence of your Creator.

If you are honest, you may discover you have a fear of being alone or being hurt. Approaching the dating scene from a place of fear will only open the door for perpetual pain, repetitive mistakes and even detrimental abuse. After completing your self-assessment, regardless of the results, pat yourself on the back for being honest with yourself and acknowledging what you need to work on.

Then you will know the truth, and the truth will set you free.
John 8:32

Often a hidden sense of self inadequacy, low self-esteem or a deeply rooted painful past causes one to feel unworthy of healthy, unconditional love. You may even feel unlovable. Do not fret my friend. The Lord instructs us thusly:

Do not be anxious about anything, but in every situation, by prayer and petition, with thanksgiving, present your requests to God.
Philippians 4:6

It is much easier to reach out than to reach within. This is why many find themselves glued into social media, fixating on the lives of others or airing out one's emotions, seeking validation, and inflating one's lifestyle. Have a real talk with God about your hurt, pain and fears. If you have experienced rape, molestation, or any form of abuse, now is your time for healing. There is no safer place than in the hands of God. Petition Him for healing and total restoration. Ask the Lord to guide you to the professional help you need towards your journey of complete rehabilitation. Begin to thank Him for the heartaches you've encountered because He is standing by to turn your worst situations into good. Forgive yourself for the mistakes you have made and the times you have dishonored yourself and God. There is nothing too hard or disappointing for God to bear, nor is there any wound too deep or secret too dark. Now is the time to confront yourself, your pain and your shame. With thanksgiving, present your requests to the Lord in faith that the best is yet to come.

See, I am doing a new thing! Now it springs up; do you not perceive it?
Isaiah 43:19

Pray with me:

Heavenly Father, please cover me with the blood of Jesus. Pour your blood over all areas that I've confronted and exposed. I ask that you begin a supernatural healing in any areas of brokenness. In your presence, there is peace. Bring light to areas of unhealthy relationships, sexuality, abuse, heartache, low self-esteem, abusive patterns or addictive behavior. Loose the chains now in Jesus' name and deliver me from any demonic interference. We surrender to your perfect will for our lives today! Old things are past. Fix what has been broken in the name of Jesus. We claim healing, deliverance and wholeness. We are victorious over our past and future. Amen.

For anyone who enters God's rest also rests from his or her works, just as God did from his.
Hebrews 4:10

Welcome to your "Season of Stillness!" If you are tired of feeling lonely, empty, and undervalued or depressed, your season of stillness is a divine invitation for healing to take place. You may be thinking there's no way God can undo the years of promiscuity or fornication in which you've participated. On the contrary, when we hand over our filthy rags to our Redeemer, not only does He heal and deliver, but He redeems. When we truly repent, our sins are forgiven and forgotten.

Who is a God like you, who pardons sin and forgives the transgression of the remnant of his inheritance? You do not stay angry forever but delight to show mercy. You will again have compassion on us; you will tread our sins underfoot and hurl all our iniquities into the depths of the sea.

Micah 7:18-19

Giving up sex can be like quitting smoking cold turkey, but with prayer and fasting you can do it! Likewise, being the odd man/woman out gets old after a while. There comes a time in the life of every virgin when you contemplate whether to compromise and just give in. If a mate is what you ultimately desire, you must first delight yourself in the company of the Lord. This was the most critical season along my celibate journey. It was this season that paved the way for my future husband to find me.

My season of stillness was needed after years of dating and seeking male attention. I was often grasping thin air, fragments of love that weren't truly there. An older friend and mentor at the time introduced me to the notion of this idea. She explained it as being a season where you allow God to be your most intimate partner. She went so far as to say when she was in her "season of stillness" God was her lover and she would sleep with her Bible. While I considered her antics rather extreme, there was truth in my spirit being desperate for time to air out and breathe. Until you get rid of the old, there will never be any room for the new.

Neither do people pour new wine into old wineskins. If they do, the skins will burst; the wine will run out and the wineskins will be ruined. No, they pour new wine into new wineskins, and both are preserved.
Matthew 9:17

Just as an earthly relationship requires time and commitment, so does your spiritual relationship with God. Think of how you respond when you have just met someone intriguing. You think about them all the time. You spend hours talking on the phone without blinking and kiss without coming up for air. Likewise, God desires to be thought of and spoken to often. When was the first or last time you spent hours with God?

Take delight in the LORD, and he will give you the desires of your heart.
Psalm 37:4

Finding rest in the Lord is opposite of the lifestyle we are accustomed to living. We are encouraged to exploit ourselves to find love. This can be downright dangerous to the one who has not gone through a season of stillness.

During this season of supernatural healing and rest, you are encouraged to take a time out from the works of your flesh. Rest from dating. Resist the urge to manufacture a relationship by your own doing. Rest your body parts. Rest your spirit. Rest your soul. Know that you can rest in the Lord. It is a sacred, intimate time. Give yourself the permission and freedom to rest and fully commit. For once, be single without seeking anyone but God. Remember, you are never alone because the One who loves you with an everlasting love is always with you to comfort and guide. Be still and know that God is God. He is above time and has everything under control. Do not be afraid of taking time to pause your dating/sex life or the preoccupation thereof. You cannot miss what God has for you.

For the Lord God is a sun and shield; the Lord bestows favor and honor; no good thing does he withhold from those whose walk is blameless.
Psalm 84:11

Do not be alarmed if you experience symptoms of withdrawal during this time. Your mind, body and soul are purging. This season is designed to rid you of your fear of loneliness and help you focus on your intimacy with God. Many of us long for a soul mate before we truly nurture the relationship with our soul's maker. God's greatest desire is for us to be in relationship with Him.

On my bed I remember you; I think of you through the watches of the night. Because you are my help, I sing in the shadow of your wings. I cling to you; your right hand upholds me. **Psalm 63:6-8**

In your "season of stillness" there are no rules, only choices that best serve your walk with God. I was already celibate when I entered my season. However, I was still making out with random guys and spending a lot of my energy thinking about dating. It was time to go to the next level of sacrifice.

You determine the length of time and stipulations for dating and having sex. However, it is highly recommended to maintain celibacy for the duration of the season. Otherwise, it's not a true time of stillness. While I did not put a definite number on how long I was committed to being still, I inherently knew I was in it for the long haul of several months or years until I felt God's hand of release. As with any major decision or fast, pray for God to prepare you to sustain it.

"He will keep you, if you want to be kept."
–Old church ladies

Pray with me:

Dear Lord thank you for being the rock that is higher than I. I know that it is only in you will I find rest for my soul. I acknowledge the decisions I have made up till this point have not been according to your perfect will. I repent for my shortcomings and for not taking heed to your word. I pray for your forgiveness. I thank you for leading me into this sacred season of stillness. Please protect my heart, cover my loins and allow me to rest for a while in you. Please remove any unfruitful relationships from my life and out of my path. Rebuke the enemy's tactics to distract and destroy my efforts to grow closer to you as I honor you with my mind, body and soul. I claim victory over my season of stillness in Jesus name! Amen.

Whoever dwells in the shelter of the Most High will rest in the shadow of the Almighty. **Psalm 91:1**

Social media keeps us locked in to the inner lives of others. However, the celibate journey requires isolation. This isolation is the perfect opportunity to develop a more intimate relationship with God. Take this time to rest and heal by immersing yourself in the presence of God. Finally, cut off people not in alignment with your goal. Don't bother wasting your time explaining why. People who are not in alignment with your purpose are not going to understand your walk. Neither will they possess the necessary tools to support you. People fear what they do not understand. Why put yourself through unnecessary grief or open yourself up to be swayed off your path?

You'll need your energy to persevere down the road less traveled.

And if your right hand causes you to stumble, cut it off and throw it away. It is better for you to lose one part of your body than for your whole body to go into hell.
Matthew 5:30

When indulging in sex, what may have started as casual play turned into mild obsession. I couldn't help wondering if I was the only one. I would be on pins and needles waiting to be acknowledged for my time, energy and affection. After a while, you get tired of expecting more than what a person is capable of.

I'm not sure what's worse, receiving physical satisfaction from someone attractive yet emotionally unavailable, or receiving a form of emotional compatibility with someone you are having sex with but still know, deep down, isn't the one. What both situations have in common is they are mismatched and out of God's order for your life. Stop entertaining the space fillers. This includes unequally yoked long term relationships. Deal with your inner voids and petition God's healing.

In keeping the 100% honesty you established in your self-check, identify your emotional and physical weaknesses. In my case, there were several people with whom I needed to sever ties. I needed to erase their numbers out of my phone and eliminate all communication with them. As a matter of fact, there were some who needed to be cut out of my life forever. Be not deceived; one text message can lead you quickly into temptation. Steer clear of dialing and texting under the influence in your season of stillness. Be smart; be vigilant and cutthroat about this. Your life and destiny are on the line, and the enemy will use any crack as an open door to tempt you to give up and turn back.

We like to keep players on the bench or "friends with benefits" in our back pocket out of comfort and security. However, if you continue to entertain past relationships, God has no room to bring in the new. This is a season of total trust. This is your time to actively wait for God's chosen mate for you. Stillness= waiting in the will of God.

Be alert and of sober mind. Your enemy the devil prowls around like a roaring lion looking for someone to devour.
1 Peter 5:8

Mr. /Mrs. Right, Right Now, Wrong

The time has come to pattern your life to receive God's best. To do this, you must begin making choices that line up with your future rather than your present. You must dedicate a portion of your life to prayer, fasting, and healing with God without someone in your life. With God on your side, you are strong enough to stand alone. I am a living witness that being alone for a while will not kill you! Sacrificing temporary pleasure and comfort is the only way to fully realize your godly potential.

I am not in the business of ending relationships, but I need to address three common traps. If God calls you into a season of stillness while you are in a relationship, listen up! You owe it to yourself to take this time for you and your personal Lord and Savior. Until your vertical relationship is solid and transparent with #1, none of your horizontal relationships will flourish. Second, it is important that you carefully assess the man/woman currently in your life. Is he Mr. /Mrs. Right, Right Now, or Wrong?

If he/she is Mr./Mrs. Right now, this may be a little challenging for you, but very possible nonetheless. Regardless of how attentive they are right now, Mr. /Mrs. Right now is not concerned with your future. More than likely he/she cannot connect with or relate to your desire to achieve deeper intimacy with God especially if that means less attention from you. Whether you want to try and explain your goals is up to you. They may not try to stop you from being celibate but they won't try and help or hold you accountable. Truth be told, they probably don't take your walk seriously.

You can gauge their reaction by assessing your level of integrity. How well do you stick by goals or honor other personal decisions in your life? If you are a fly by night person who changes your mind each time the wind blows and doesn't normally follow through with your goals, do not expect Mr. /Mrs. Right Now to take you seriously.

Mr. or Mrs. Right Now is primarily concerned with their needs right now. They talk a good game and go along with what you want as long as they get their end of the bargain. You are only responsible for expressing the choices you have resolved to take, not the reasons for wanting to make that choice. It's possible you will have to cut him or her off cold turkey, no questions asked or answered. Just let them know you can no longer continue seeing him/her, for personal reasons, and wish them well. Your priority is nurturing your spiritual health and relationship with God.

Whenever you feel tempted to reach out to him/her or answer their calls, remind yourself you are doing this for God, your Heavenly Father, the one who loves you unconditionally and will give you all that you need in His perfect timing. Honestly, Mr. Right Now, is far too tempting to keep around in your season of stillness. More than likely, he appeals to all of your senses and most of your weaknesses. Mr. Right Now is the perfect space filler that can deliver the "goods" and get you to your sexual peak, not later but right now.

However, until you release Mr. /Mrs. Right Now, God can't fully prepare you for Mr. Right. If you are serious about seeking God for wholeness and to present you with Mr. Right, get rid of Mr. Right Now! After all, they are not your husband/wife and you need time to physically and spiritually purge from them. You don't want memories of your sexual past haunting your future marriage. Why settle for partial fulfillment when God has the man/woman of your destiny waiting in the wings to help you achieve your divine purpose? In preparing to enter a season of stillness, give yourself a hand by removing distractions. Mr. Right Now is often the most enticing of distractions. Mr. Right Now will have a bruised ego, but he'll let you go and find his next friend with benefits. Kiss him/her "Buh-bye."

Now to Mr. Wrong. You may be wondering what the difference is since Mr. Right now is wrong as well. Mr. Right Now isn't necessarily awful for you; he just doesn't line up with your future and thus, can't make the final cut. There is only one spot for Mr. Right. It is only Mr. Right who will not have you do anything to compromise your spirit. Mr. Wrong on the other hand makes you compromise your inner convictions in more ways than one. He is detrimental to you either physically, mentally, or spiritually. He very well may be a glorious combination of all detriments. Mr. Wrong has no interest in whether you are in God's will right now or ever. In fact, he is a big part of what has you feeling more disconnected to God than ever before.

This may not be your first experience with allowing yourself to be part of an unhealthy relationship. Mr. Wrong has disrespected you on one or more occasion. Yet for some reason you allow him to continue filling a void in your life. If you're anything like me, you've convinced yourself that Mr. Wrong is Mr. Right and hoping one day he will learn to love you the right way. You've already given so much of yourself, it's hard to imagine what it will take to detach yourself and start anew.

Beware! When you communicate your decision with Mr. Wrong, I can almost guarantee he will respond in the wrong way. Mr. Wrong is incredibly insecure and delusional. He will not understand. He will take it personally and do whatever he can to keep his power over you and maintain the upper hand. Be prepared for him to pull out all the stops. He will bring his highest levels of manipulation to the table and do whatever he can to reel you back in. If you cut him off without explanation, at worst, he'll become volatile and stalk you. At best, he'll just assume you will be back.

They say all addicts come to their senses and realize they need to make a change once they've hit rock bottom. Let this be your warning. If you are with Mr. Wrong, honey, you have already hit rock bottom and have had many warnings. Your spirit has already given you a gentle nudge and told you you've had enough yet you feel too weak to leave. For some, your spirit has been screaming for help and you are denying yourself the freedom and peace you need and deserve. Perhaps you do not value yourself enough to think you deserve or will ever receive better. Wipe the fog off the bathroom mirror.

Recognize the spirit looking back at you, suffocating in all the steam from the hot shower.

This is exactly the place the enemy wants to keep you. If you are living in this type of oppression, you will remain in a mental prison. Open the bathroom door and let the steam come out. God wants to set you free today! You were created to live a life of peace, joy and fulfillment from a partner. God will not bring anyone in your life that will ask you to compromise His will. With that, you have the power to live your life with a clean slate. Begin praying for the strength to walk away from Mr. Wrong once and for all.

The tough part is Mr. Wrong almost always provides something that's oh so right. It could be sex, money or just time and attention. If you are relying on Mr. Wrong for food, clothing, shelter or emotional stability, you must be willing to go without. The Season of Stillness is about resting in God and relying totally on Him for your needs and wants. Ask God to be your sole provider. He has been waiting for you to come to your senses and turn back to Him. This is not by any means an easy step. Until you fully surrender to God, you will always be indebted to Mr. Wrong. Mr. Wrong is not the lover of your soul. Only Christ can be that if you allow Him.

If we truly believed in God's unconditional undying love for us, we would never entertain Mr. Wrong. Allow Christ to be everything you need, even your "Sugar

Daddy/Mamma". In the meantime, you must cultivate a healthy self-esteem and love yourself. Discern which thoughts you are hearing that are of God and which are from the enemy. God loves you and wants you to be filled with His love. His arms are big enough to protect you. Uproot the negative things people have said about you and your future. Allow your mind to be renewed by His word.

Ask God to reveal your innermost fears about letting go and remaining pure. For me, I was afraid of being alone. If sex is what it took to keep companionship, I was game. I also had a false sense of entitlement and an inflated ego. I felt entitled to love, companionship and even sex. This sense of entitlement led me into awkward interactions and regretful experiences.

Many are the plans in a person's heart, but it is the LORD's purpose that prevails.
Proverbs 19:21

If sex and a need for physical touch are too difficult for you to quit cold turkey, try fasting. I recommend you fast one day a week until you get stronger. On the day you choose to fast, eliminate sex, pornography, phone calls, text messages, social media, explicit music and even TV. Some people have more toxic habits and powerful strongholds than others, but you have the power to change! Even though it may not feel this way, the power of God dwelling within you is more power than the allure and temptation of sex.

You, dear children, are from God and have overcome them, because the one who is in you is greater than the one who is in the world. **1 John 4:4**

Setting Boundaries

When I was engaging in sex outside of marriage, I subconsciously made a firm case to justify my behavior. After all, a young, attractive woman is entitled to having and entertaining suitors, right? Perhaps according to the world, but God has a much higher standard intended for our highest good. Buying into the lie the world was telling me about being in control of my own sexuality sanctioned me to be free and find pleasure in justifying sin. I was walking in the alluring fantasy of darkness.

If the relationship was exclusive and I could see this person (in my vain imagination) being my life long partner, sex before marriage was no longer "that bad of a sin". Although having one casual one night stand left me feeling used and broken, I told myself, "Everyone should be free-spirited enough to experience this at least once." Over time, telling me this repeatedly distanced me from the reality of my sin consciousness and weakened the conviction of the Holy Spirit. Although the Holy Spirit made it nearly impossible for me to find true peace, lying to myself about the reality of sin made it easier to live according to the world's way rather than God's.

We demolish arguments and every pretension that sets itself up against the knowledge of God, and we take captive every thought to make it obedient to Christ.
2 Corinthians 10:5

As a woman, I subconsciously thought of sex as a duty. I believed it was my obligation to please whatever man was in my life at the time to keep his attention. Many times, women are not able to walk in celibacy because of low self-esteem disguised as heightened sexuality. We are more afraid of losing a man than we are afraid of displeasing our heavenly Father.

Another trap that keeps us in the dark while in sexually active relationships is a sense of deprivation. We long for constant validation from the opposite sex. It is not until we fill ourselves up with the knowledge of God and allow Him to fill our void that we will be in position to receive God's best. I can safely say, having sex never resulted in me receiving the pure emotional connection and spiritual compatibility I was longing for.

I used to think giving a sacred piece of myself to a man would cause him to return the favor by giving more of himself to me and fall head over heels. Don't get me wrong, at times my intentions were strictly physical. However, even in those select cases, I was aware I had shared the deepest part of myself. Whether I wanted to voluntarily open my soul or not, the door had been open and I was choosing to keep my eyes closed. This is what we do when we engage in sex and tell ourselves "our feelings aren't involved and it's just sex." We close our eyes and begin lying to ourselves about the reality of soul ties. Each time we lay down with another, our soul becomes tied to them in some way. Having sex without emotional attachment is very dangerous because not only are you not living according to God's Word, you aren't being 100% honest with yourself. It's easy to peg someone a "sex toy", but you are indeed sharing your soul with another.

If you are truly honest, and you looked a person in the eye before you were about to have sex and declared "I'm about to share my soul with you and I expect love, exclusivity, respect and validation" you would stop dead in your tracks knowing this person is not right or worthy of having the depths of you. Choosing to take a blind eye to the reality of creating a soul tie with another individual is not healthy and will lead to more dishonesty in other areas of your life.

Light

Sin (the dirtiest word of all) is anything that separates us from God. To be successful in celibacy, you must be willing to walk in the light. Become totally transparent with God, yourself and potential mates. Sugar coating and justifying disobedience is not going to serve you ultimately.

Celibacy is a form of spiritual nakedness. Abstinence allows us to operate in truth and light. God as the center and true headship is the foundation of any God-ordained marriage. Be not deceived, the enemy will allow us to find false comfort in fulfilling relationships while engaging in premarital sex. By picking and choosing areas of obedience according to the Word, we are selling ourselves short and missing out on the fullness of abundant living. However, it is not until sex is taken out of the equation that we see ourselves as we truly are and see our partners as they truly are.

Walking in the light means remaining conscious in all your decisions. Only make decisions that support your goal. For example, if your goal is to grow your hair out it doesn't make sense to keep cutting it shorter and shorter. You'll start eating foods that promote healthy growth and cultivate the patience required to get to your desired length. Why settle for being a lifelong "friend", baby mama, or girlfriend when you truly desire to become a wife? If the relationship is truly ordained by God, your partner will respect your decision to wait while making the necessary sacrifices to turn over a new leaf of abstinence with you.

If you're walking in truth, you must learn to set healthy boundaries that will serve your highest good. Pray for discernment to dictate what situations you should flee from. It isn't wise to mix alcohol or other drugs when you're dating new people. Spending the night out of convenience may be too risky for where you currently are on your journey. Why push the limits when your integrity is on the line? You may just need to take a break from online dating. Heck, delete your profile for a while. Keep an open dialogue with God every step of the way. Hold yourself accountable and keep walking.

You set the barometer. As you grow stronger, your boundaries will change. Don't be afraid to talk to God about your weaknesses. He's standing by to support your walk, not judge you. As children of God, we are to rise up to the standard of our Father, not twist biblical teachings to accommodate our lifestyles. Along the road, I had to decline an invitation from an eligible bachelor who was surprisingly OK with my decision to remain celibate to go to Jamaica. I had no doubt we'd have a great time and I may have even been able to hold out. However, I knew I had the tendency to submit to having sex out of obligation and I knew this man wasn't my husband. Furthermore, this wasn't a honeymoon, so I had to say no. Saying NO to the hard things is in fact saying yes to God.

Believing that the Bible no longer applies or is no longer relevant because the standard seems entirely too high is a trick of the enemy. God encourages us to be in the world but not of the world. I was later able to go on many vacations with the man who is now my husband who just so happens to be Jamaican. I'm glad I held out. I don't have to say, "I've been there before with some guy". My first trip there will be with him.

Protection

While the world will say you need to have sex with anyone you're serious about marrying to see if you are sexually compatible, having sex prematurely leaves a permanent imprint in your mind of past experiences that can be very difficult to erase (whether good or bad). Celibacy helps purge us from experience and somewhat free our minds from sexual encounters that can later put a damper on intimacy in marriage.

Our obedience to God protects us from unseen snares of the enemy. Once again, God sets the standard to protect us, not to punish. I'm not saying walking down the road less traveled is an easy one. But the path of light leads to eternal life. God is your sunblock! He is your protection. He sets the standard for your highest good by bringing glory to Him. While we are focused on the present moment, what feels good now, God is focused on your life bringing glory to Him and your eternal destiny.

Contrary to popular belief, no matter how beautiful, gifted or educated you are, your life is not your own. You belong to God. The world encourages us to be young, wild and free. So much so, we've been deceived into believing we have a right to do what we wish with our bodies. From Instagram booties to racy sex scenes on network television, we are flooded with images of sexual exploitation and immorality daily.

Make no mistake:

Do you not know that your bodies are temples of the Holy Spirit, who is in you, whom you have received from God? You are not your own.
-1 Corinthians 6:19

There are countless physical and spiritual benefits to being celibate—protection from a multitude of consequences like unwanted pregnancy, abortion and toxic soul ties to name a few. Not to mention S.T.Ds (sexually transmitted diseases) and what's worse, **sexually transmitted demons**.

You are a slave of the one you obey, whether that be a slave to sin which leads to death or a slave to obedience which leads to righteousness.
Romans 6:16

Once you've made the decision to engage in the deepest level of human intimacy, be aware of the territory you're entering. You're physically and spiritually merging your soul with another. You're open to them activating your own dormant demons and vulnerable to picking up any physical or spiritual ailments your sexual partner is carrying. Increased depression, numbness, clinginess, an unhealthy desire to please, preoccupation, obsession, anger, heightened sexuality, or even sexual addiction are all symptoms of sexually transmitted demons.

The enemy is looking for whom he can devour. Therefore, God places much importance on fleeing from temptation. There is so much happening in the unseen realm. While a person may look attractive on the outside, sex blinds us from seeing the demons that could be in operation on the inside.

While I'd like to think my celibate journey began once I maintained a blameless walk, I think it began a bit before. About two years prior to becoming celibate (without falling), I'd made a concerted effort in my mind. I was trying to cut ties with the old flame who was still hitting me up. One night, he caught me in a moment of weakness. I was in the middle of a trying quarter during graduate school. My days and nights were filled with classes, performances and seeing the same nine classmates day after day. I needed an escape and a moment of release. I still hadn't gotten him out of my system.

At this point, I was open with my relationship with God. I knew this guy was battling some inner demons and in the midst of my fornication, I was even trying to gently plant seeds of God's saving grace. Perhaps I was acting as a wolf in sheep's clothing. In the middle of our conversation, his roommate was in the other room being a little loud and unruly (nothing out of the norm when living with roommates). The next thing I knew, he hopped out of his bed, pulled out a gun and stood behind the door cursing and yelling at his roommate to be quiet. I entered a state of panic and my heart began to race. To this day, I'll never understand what in the devil had gotten into him or what's worse, what I had allowed to enter me. He could have snapped and turned the gun on me as I lay naked underneath the sheets.

Needless to say, this was a major red flag. I was supposed to be practicing celibacy! After calming him down, I quickly made a run for it. I'm not sure if the drive home was so foggy because of the southern California smog or the flood of tears impeding my vision. I'd done it again and this time, it could've cost me my life.

While the grace of God often protects us even during sin, every choice we make comes with a consequence be it good or bad. It only takes one encounter to create a lifelong problem. Pre-marital sex opens us up to the devil's domain. A moment of physical gratification isn't worth the gamble. This was a sign from God that although I was trying, I was now playing with fire.

Whether we are young, old, having casual sex, or in a committed relationship, ANY sex outside of marriage takes us out of God's perfect will. Sex can make you stay in a relationship God never intended you to be in. On our own, letting go of sex may seem impossible. God has not set any standard too high for us to fulfill. With the help of the Holy Spirit, all things are possible.

Instead of looking at God's protection as we would an over-protective Father of whom we need to rebel against, look at His protection as one of the blessed benefits of being saved.

I'll end this chapter with my final hoorah before the success of my six-year stint of celibacy. Unfortunately for me, I had to hit rock bottom before I could be successfully committed for the long haul.

I developed a crush on my long standing male best friend who was also a talented actor and trusted mentor. In hindsight, I cannot fully blame him for the chain of unfortunate events that would ensue since I played a key part in escalating our untainted friendship to a place it never should have gone. Therefore, being fully honest with yourself is a key part of healing and overcoming. We are in charge of our bodies and must take responsibility for everything we allow to dishonor ourselves. Had I only remained faithful to God, I could have spared myself weeks of feeling physically ill and years of harboring resentment and un-forgiveness towards him.

This young man was a man of God and an amazing friend. Dating a Christian does not justify sin. He was a charming, witty intellect. We'd met at a study abroad program in England. We would spend countless hours talking about everything under the sun (mainly because he loved to hear himself talk). Over the years, he understood me on a level most guys up to this point couldn't. Instead of allowing God to lead, I took this friendship as a sign he could be my soul mate.

Although I vowed to God the gun encounter would be my last until marriage, I was desperate to shower someone with my love and fidelity. I began keeping the Mary J. Blige song, "Seven Days" on heavy rotation. All I can say is five minutes of intercourse left me with an STD, by God's grace, an impermanent, very treatable one. However, this was rock bottom for me. While I was educated and talented I'd broken my vow to God. What hurt the most was I trusted him and I was so caught up in how much I trusted our friendship, I didn't use protection. I was left facing the truth of the matter: I wanted him to love me more than I loved myself and had officially stepped out of the incubator of God's protection.

Integrity

Complete the good work you've made up in your mind to achieve! Those who've achieved great success in any area have mastered the principle of integrity. Integrity is defined as the state of being whole and undivided. Making up your mind is the first step. Integrity is remaining steadfast in your decision simply because you said you would. While it came after hitting an all-time low, once I cultivated this principle, nothing could stop me from staying faithful to my first love, God.

When the Holy Spirit comes upon you, you shall receive power! Whatever weaknesses are in your flesh and sexual demons you battle, God is raising the standard against the enemy.

When the enemy shall come in like a flood, the Spirit of the Lord shall lift a standard against him.
Isaiah 59:19

As you surrender to Christ, the chains of lust, sexual addiction, and fear of being alone fall off. God is calling you to a place of Holiness in perfect union with Him. Not only is it possible, it is tangible. Reach within and tune into the powerful spirit of God living within you. You can do all things through Christ who strengthens you. This process tremendously raised the level of my personal integrity and restored my damaged self-esteem.

Integrity is the quality or state of being complete or undivided and firm to a code of especially moral or artistic values. A virtuous human being must have integrity which begins with self-trust. The virtuous characteristic of integrity begins as a small seed planted on the inside, later producing bountiful fruit that will spill over into all areas of your life.

Making the decision to be celibate is first a commitment to God that only you can fulfill. How can you whole heartedly commit to another before whole heartedly committing to God and then yourself? Like many people in my situation, I was tentative about taking on this sacred vow because of my many failed attempts.

At this point, my head was hanging low. I barely trusted myself to finish what I'd begun. However, God remembered my vow and heaven was in my corner. These setbacks were setting me up for victory.

Lowering personal standards for the sake of attention, affection and physical gratification can negatively affect your self-esteem. Taking control of your actions and holding yourself accountable is a great step towards cultivating amazing self-esteem. I had to own the fact that I allowed myself to trust a man more than I trusted God. Had I remained obedient under the shadow of the Almighty, God's protection would have prevented me from living with the consequences of contracting that Godforsaken STD and damaging a wonderful friendship.

Self-esteem is not just approving one's outer appearance, but understanding and nurturing your inner value. How much can a person trust someone who never keeps his or her word? Not very much. After a while they become like the boy who cried wolf. You don't believe anything they say and ultimately lose total respect.

Celibacy heightened the level of my personal integrity and yielded much fruit. My integrity became undoubtedly apparent after looking up one day and realizing that with God's help I was capable of staying true to my commitment and of honoring myself. Boy, was that an accomplished feeling. I could look in the mirror with pride and purity. Pleasing God isn't always easy, but in the end it gives life, joy, and peace more abundantly. Standing on the principle of integrity provides an even more positive sense of self-worth rooted in love, not pride or ego.

Going against God and looking for love our own way can lead to misery. Trust Him and remain steadfast until He elevates you to marriage. Watch your integrity blossom like never before. This overflowing integrity will trickle over into your business and personal relationships. Knowing that you are capable of keeping your word to yourself is a gift from God, yielding strength, power and authority to practice integrity in all facets of your life!

Know your triggers and create boundaries

Once your integrity is checked, allow your decision to become celibate to liberate your dating experiences. Being celibate does not mean you cannot still date and have fun. In fact, it allows dating to be more fun and empowering. Instead of giving your power away, you are now honing it. You are allowing yourself to air out your past and rest your body and soul. You are truly healing and really giving yourself the opportunity to get to know someone. Women, a lot of times think, "A grown man with needs is not going to wait for me to have sex". I was even told this a time or two when I vocalized my stance. Once I'd maintained my integrity by standing firm in my commitment to obey God, I knew I was worth the wait. God was weeding out the "rif-raff"

Do not conform to the pattern of this world, but be transformed by the renewing of your mind. Then you will be able to test and approve what God's will is--his good, pleasing and perfect will.

Romans 12:2

Now that some of the external clutter is out of your way and you have begun fortifying your self-esteem, start journaling. In your sacred quiet time make a list of all relationships and sexual partners. Go back to where you were emotionally, when you allowed each partner into your life. Write about the experiences. What was good, bad, and what did you learn? You will see that maybe not all your experiences were bad and that you learned a great amount about yourself and life in the process. Take note of the behavioral patterns. Were men or women ever a crutch or used as a void or a mask covering something deeper? Did drugs/alcohol influence any of your decisions? Most importantly, revisit your relationship with God throughout the years and over the course of your life's journey. This is your time of purging and healing. Cry when you need to cry, scream when you feel angry, take some time to go to the beach or have a bonfire. Write out all the painful experiences and names of people who hurt you whether it was voluntary or involuntary hurt. Take responsibility for your part in the pain. Forgive yourself. Forgive your abusers. Say a prayer of release and throw those pieces of paper into the ocean or into the fire and let them go. You are on your way to wholeness. Be still and rest in the Lord.

It is vital that you replace old negative habits with positive ones. Idle time will cause you to regress. Take the time to nurture your gifts and inner passions. Now that you have more free time on your hands, pick up a new hobby and finally complete the tasks you've been putting on hold. Your season of stillness is all about you. Make yourself feel good. Take yourself out to a movie or a nice dinner and bring a good book to keep you company. Write letters of gratitude to your friends and family. Create a daily practice of spending time with God by talking to Him. Meditate on His Word, words of affirmation and truth. The spiritual food you eat during this time will begin to plant seeds that will later grow plentiful fruit that will remain. Change and restoration are a process. Do not be in a hurry to exit your "Season of Stillness".

Begin meditating and speaking these affirmations to strengthen your heart:

When I doubt myself or my walk, "God has awesome plans for my future."

For I know the plans I have for you, declares the LORD, plans for welfare and not for evil, to give you a future and a hope. **Jeremiah 29:11**

Although heartbroken, "Even when man is not, God is faithful to me."

Know therefore that the LORD your God is God, the faithful God who keeps covenant and steadfast love with those who love him and keep his commandments, to a thousand generations. **Deuteronomy 7:9**

While I'm waiting, "I am not forgotten."

Can a woman forget her nursing child, that she should have no compassion on the son of her womb? Even these may forget, yet I will not forget you. **Isaiah 49:15**

I'm no longer a prisoner to sin. "Christ really does live in me."

I have been crucified with Christ. It is no longer I who live, but Christ who lives in me. And the life I now live in the flesh I live by faith in the Son of God, who loved me and gave himself for me. **Galatians 2:20**

I do not need to pursue the affection of man. "God's love for me is the greatest love of all."

Greater love has no one than this that someone lay down his life for his friends. **John 15:13**

My past does not dictate my future. "I am being transformed for the better."

And we, who with unveiled faces all reflect the Lord's glory, are being transformed into his likeness with ever-increasing glory, which comes from the Lord, who is the Spirit.
2 Corinthians 3:18

Although I've not always respected my value, I am purposed for greatness. "I was created by God to do great things."

For we are God's workmanship, created in Christ Jesus to do good works, which God prepared in advance for us to do.
Ephesians 2:10

My sins are no longer. "I am a new creation in Christ and cannot be held to my past."

Therefore, if anyone is in Christ, he is a new creation; the old has gone, the new has come! **2 Corinthians 5:17**

"I am a friend of the highest God."

I no longer call you servants…Instead, I have called you friends, for everything that I learned from my Father I have made known to you. **John 15:15**

I'm equipped to complete my race with victory because "God has chosen me."

You did not choose me, but I chose you and appointed you to go and bear fruit—fruit that will last. Then the Father will give you whatever you ask in my name. **John 15:16**

"I have God's approval."

He appointed us, set his seal of ownership on us, and put his Spirit in our hearts as a deposit, guaranteeing what is to come. **2 Corinthians 1:21-22**

Despite my weaknesses, "I have the strength to be successful in celibacy."

I can do everything through him [Christ] who gives me strength. **Philippians 4:13**

I do not have to walk in condemnation because "God has forgiven me."

Blessed is the man whose sin the Lord will never count against him. **Romans 4:8**

"Guilt doesn't belong in my life."

Therefore, there is now no condemnation for those who are in Christ Jesus. **Romans 8:1**

"I am free."

So if the Son sets you free [from sin], you will be free indeed. **John 8:36**

"Nothing can separate me from the love of God"

For I am convinced that neither death nor life, neither angels nor demons, neither the present nor the future, nor any powers, neither height nor depth, nor anything else in all creation, will be able to separate us from the love of God that is in Christ Jesus our Lord. **Romans 8:38-39**

"I will continue to set my mind on eternal things."

Set your minds on things above, not on earthly things. For you died, and your life is now hidden with Christ in God. When Christ, who is your life, appears, then you also will appear with him in glory. Put to death, therefore, whatever belongs to your earthly nature: sexual immorality, impurity, lust, evil desires and greed, which is idolatry? **Colossians 3:2-5**

"God has promises for my obedience"

Hear, Israel, and be careful to obey so that it may go well with you and that you may increase greatly in a land flowing with milk and honey, just as the Lord, the God of your ancestors, promised you. **Deuteronomy 6:3**

CHANNELING YOUR ENERGY

Energy can neither be created nor destroyed, but it can be transferred. Aha!

Bringing your body under subjection may first feel like taming a wild beast. It's normal to experience feelings of dejection or defeat for having to say no to what feels natural. Hold your head high for you are a child of God and of a royal priesthood. Channel your energy towards pride and confidence that you've been enlightened and are now in walking in spiritual alignment. This is where miracles take place and transformation occurs.

Masturbation

Celibacy is a journey. The church seldom addresses the topic of masturbation. For good reason, since it's very uncomfortable to talk about. Some will argue it's a healthy form of self-exploration. While there is some truth to this, masturbation is a sticky slope that can quickly turn into addiction and create distance in our relationship with God. It's always an easily accessible outlet to channel sexual energy. While I do not have a Scripture to directly address the topic of masturbation, bringing our bodies under subjection is about starving the flesh fully. I will first say hats off to those who are able to remain celibate without masturbating. That is unfortunately not my story. There were times when masturbation felt like the only alternative. While this is not the worst thing you can do while remaining celibate, it's not the best. I say this because masturbation is a solo act. God intended sex to be in communion with another. Masturbation also invites entrance into the fantasy world. Invoking a spirit of lust can open the door to more sex and a different type of stronghold. God doesn't intend for us to give up sex in the light while we remain sex-crazed maniacs in the dark.

We must be very careful about the images we allow to enter our eyes and ears. Masturbating is like fanning an already lit fire. You think fanning the flame would put the fire out, but it in turn makes the fire grow. Masturbation lets off steam in the moment, but turning to pornography or imagining past or imaginary lovers is not living up to God's best. How do I know this? It's not something you'd be proud of doing in the presence of God. The celibate journey is about taming our flesh while in pursuit of God's best. If this is an area of struggle for you, try fasting from masturbation as often as you can until you are able to fully let go. If you are unable to tackle this alone, seek out an anonymous support group for help. God wants us to gain discipline over our bodies, which includes masturbation.

I had a friend ask me if I was ever able to give up masturbation or did it get me through to the end. My best answer was to use an analogy related to being vegan. If you've ever met a strict vegan, they are serious about not eating any animal products whatsoever. Some of these people slowly integrated themselves into the vegan lifestyle by cutting out one animal product at a time until they became fully vegan. Vegans take great pride in what they put into their bodies. They are unwilling to eat anything they deem toxic. My celibate journey was very similar. I had to slowly let go of patterns of behavior not in alignment with God's best. Over time, I lost the urge to disobey God. My discernment had increased. I wasn't interested in taking on the spirits of another and risk catching a sexually transmitted demon. I had spent too much time purging, healing and renewing my mind in Christ. After time, as the vegan looks at meat, I began to despise the act of sex outside of God's intended purpose as I knew it wasn't for my highest good. The Holy Spirit was transforming my mind, making it more like Christ.

This concept becomes easier to walk out when you focus less on getting rid of your urges and more on channeling them. The more you feed your mind with vulgar music, pornography, late night texting, or whatever fuels the flame of temptation, the more difficult it will be to stay the course. For example, if your goal is to lose weight you're going to want to steer clear of the "Hot" Krispy Crème sign.

On a natural level, find healthy ways to channel your sexual energy. Exercise, yoga, and mediation are great places to begin. Becoming more in tune with the mind, body, and spirit connection encourages more empowered, conscious decision making. Sex is nothing more than a stimulation of the senses. Yet, we have the freedom to explore our senses without having sex. For instance, cooking with natural, organic foods can be an invigorating experience, enlivening all your senses. Exploring the touch, smell and flavor of different foods and spices can help channel your feel-good vibes. Plus, it's a great way to entertain a group of friends when you feel like having company instead of hooking up with a random person from a dating site or calling an ex over for "Netflix and chill" (yeah right).

Physical activity is the perfect way to replace the occasional impatience or lethargy that accompanies a celibate lifestyle. Going for a run and feeling the wind blow while breathing and letting go of any pent-up energy can leave you feeling more relaxed while keeping you headed in the right direction. Joining a group fitness class that pushes you while getting human interaction is also a great way to channel pent up sexual energy.

This may sound crazy, but trying out different fabrics and exploring how they feel on your skin or experiencing with how different oils/fragrances make you feel throughout the day opens your senses and allows you to feel good about simply existing in your own skin without co-dependency on another.

Perhaps none of these alternatives seem practical for you. The goal is to replace an unhealthy behavior with a healthier substitute. Remember you're not saying no forever. This is just a season. At the end, you'll not only have increased your self-esteem but you'll become more self-aware. If you're addicted to the thrill of fornicating, find a new, healthier thrill. Perhaps try an extreme sport or embark upon a new adventure. If you're allured by the secrecy that comes along with disobeying God, find other activities you can do alone.

For example, after I became a new mom I would sneak and have a cigarette every now and then to have some alone time and reclaim my personal space. When I felt the addiction of smoking trying to take hold, I realized I was more addicted to the habit. I was addicted to the behavior of going outside and looking up into the sky, breathing in and out in solitude. I was able to replace the behavior of smoking with sitting outside, looking up at the sky and breathing in out without the cigarettes and I'd bring a good book to fill up the empty space.

If the above still sounds ridiculous to you or adversely prompts you to act upon your sexual desires, you'll have to take a more aggressive approach which comes only by prayer and fasting. Begin incorporating fasting and prayer into your weekly routine. Dedicate one day out of the week to cutting out the triggers that activate your sexual behavior. This may include disconnecting from social media, dating sites, pornography, and dating. Anyone can do just about anything for one day. If you can't go one day, start with a half a day or even one hour. Start where you are and replace your triggers with prayer.

Being celibate doesn't stop us from having sexual urges. In fact, we were created to be sexual beings, in the proper context with one ordained person. It's a hard pill to swallow but it's our job to control our bodies until our due season of marriage. Instead of asking God to remove the desire to have sex, ask for the patience to wait and the temperament to control your body. It truly gets easier with time. After all, there is nothing more attractive than a man with self-control and a woman who knows her worth.

Some are unwilling to try being celibate because of the old saying, "If you don't use it, you'll lose it". Do you see now how lies such as this are not of God?

For the spirit God gave us does not make us timid, but gives us power, love and self-discipline.
2 Timothy 1:7

With self-control comes a change in the power your sexuality has over you. There was a time I felt my desire for sex was a beast I had to feed. If I'm totally honest, every encounter wasn't even all that pleasurable! Once I placed my body under subjection to the Holy Spirit, by the end of my 6-year celibate journey, I experienced a level of self-control I never imagined possible where even masturbation no longer had a hold.

For some, this hot flame turned cool water can be frightening out of fear that you've lost the desire to ever have sex again. For me, it took time to give myself the freedom to channel everything I'd been storing up. The more you focus on self-care the more you'll value your worth and will realize you are too valuable a prize to compromise God's perfect plans for your future. Explore healthy alternatives to taking care of yourself by showering yourself with the attention you're seeking on the outside.

Getting up If You Fall

As I stated before, my journey consisted of falling off and being confronted with my bloody wounds before I processed the enormity of remaining on the celibate wagon for the long haul. Remember, once you have the Holy Spirit, you have already received power. You've already been offered compassion, forgiveness and power. While it grieves the Holy Spirit when we choose to disobey God, our loving Father is not standing by to punish you if you disobey. The Holy Spirit does not condemn, He corrects. He wants you to repent (turn back to Him), accept His forgiveness and keep walking in His power.

If you've fallen after taking on the sacred vow of celibacy, take a step back and first repent. Resist the temptation to justify your actions and immediately go into a few days of prayer and fasting. Even when you fall, God remains in your corner. The enemy is seeking to keep you in bondage. Do not punish yourself. Identify any thoughts of justification but don't waste time and energy condemning yourself. Wipe your tears and keep walking.

Acknowledge the fact you made the decision to gratify your flesh. Write about what triggered your decision, and how you felt after the encounter. Depending on how long you've been out of step with the Holy Spirit, you may feel better behaving badly before you feel worse.

Once you've accepted Christ, trust Him to be your compass and stop ignoring your innermost convictions. While your body and mind may be saying just go for it, if you allow yourself to get quiet, dig a little deeper and listen a little longer you'll hear the Shephard telling you to keep waiting. We often give in when we think God is saying NO forever. Remember, this is just a season and this too shall pass. Remain in the presence of God and continue declaring His promises over your life. Rise above falling into guilt or condemnation and do not allow the enemy to convince you that just because you've given in you have to continue. Jesus already died for this moment.

Keep going with God. If you decide you want to get a little more out of your system, don't make excuses. Instead, be honest with yourself and God that you are willfully choosing disobedience for this moment in time and pray for God to remove the lust and desire you don't want to let go of.

Celibate and in a Relationship

The saying is true, "Why buy the cow when you can get the milk for free?" This chapter is pertinent to those who've gone through all the former stages and are now in courtship with someone believed to be ordained by God. Or, for those who've been having pre-marital sex in a committed relationship for quite some time but the light of marriage seems far in the distant future.

I would be lying if I said I didn't hug, kiss or test the limits with my husband while we were courting. We even came close to giving in. However, when confronted with the decision whether to give in, I was reminded of the vow I made to God. Moreover, I was reminded of the wisdom given by Dr. Najuma Smith Pollard, "You don't just fall into bed with someone, you make the decision." I knew I had to hold myself accountable and I'd come too far to turn back. By the grace of God, we had cultivated the self-restraint to not cross the line. This may or may not be the case for you. Seek the Lord for the level of intimacy you're able to handle prior to your wedding night.

What is intimacy? Intimacy is defined as a close, familiar and affectionate personal relationship. Intimacy is an act of expression serving as a token of familiarity or affection. In the Garden of Eden, God created Adam and Eve to be in a harmonious relationship with Him. It is human nature to desire intimacy and affection on a deeply spiritual level based upon the way we are biologically wired. God created Adam and Eve to enjoy the fruits of the garden and they were permitted to satisfy one another, naked before God. They had already been joined together before God, which is in today's terms likened to a modern-day wedding ceremony.

We are created to enjoy intimacy and physical gratification with another. Why would God give us these longings and physical needs to make us wait and hold out? For everything there is a season. Do not ask God to take your natural desires away, but ask Him to help you control them until your due season of marriage before God.

Like Adam and Eve, we as humans rely more on our physical longings and human wisdom than our spiritual discernment and commitment towards obeying God. Before drawing conclusions about what can be done for intimacy and figuring out which corners can be cut to enjoy intimacy without going all the way, let's examine several fundamental truths about God's expectations.

Therefore, I urge you, brothers and sisters, in view of God's mercy, to offer your bodies as a living sacrifice, holy and pleasing to God-this is your true and proper worship.
Romans 12:1

Sacrifice

Firstly, God recognizes the choice to become/remain celibate a sacrifice. Jesus Christ Himself walked the Earth as a man, so He is not in the dark about the physical needs of a man. Yet, he walked the Earth without sin. While we will never be perfect like Christ, as we believeth on Him to gain access to the tree of eternal life, there is a level of submission we are expected to live by. The Scripture says, "I beseech ye therefore brethren by the mercies of God." the keyword being "mercies". Mercy is compassion or forgiveness shown toward someone whom it is within one's power to punish or harm.

Celibacy is an event to be grateful for and excited about. Go into it with gratitude for the compassion and forgiveness you have. Before presenting your body as a living sacrifice, realize God has already extended His mercies. Mercy in the plural equals compassion and forgiveness repeatedly.

The body craves physical touch and the mind is curious. God knows we will not always hit the mark, which is why He says I beseech you by the mercies of God. We are not expected to take on such a sacrifice without God's compassion and forgiveness. There are many things God could have requested as a sacrifice (money, belongings, time etc.) However, the sacrifice God wants is our bodies. How wonderful is it that the Bible acknowledges the presentation of the body as a sacrifice? Sex is something we want to hold onto but we give it up for a greater good.

Sacrifice is an act of slaughtering an animal or person or surrendering a possession as an offering to God. The decision to abstain from sex is a sacrifice mandated and honored by God. When God asked Abraham to "sacrifice" his son, he knew that was the closest thing to his heart and would require much faith and trust. Likewise, whenever God asks us to "sacrifice" something he knows it is a difficult act of utter surrender. God knows choosing celibacy goes against the very fiber of our being. But when it comes to our bodies, God requires both. After all, our bodies are His living temple. Your body is the living sacrifice God is after. He has already extended mercies because he knows this level of obedience will require a supernatural way of life. Resisting the natural to obtain a deeper supernatural connection and power. Resisting the fleeting physical gratifications of human intercourse for what is unseen and often lonely requires a deeper and closer walk with Christ.

God knows something about sacrifice himself. He gave His only son to the world to save you from your sins. We are free to obey and love God because He first loved us. It is important to consider how deep the Father's love is for us and how intimate we have become with Him before considering what levels of intimacy are appropriate.

After considering God's thoughts regarding you and your body being presented as a living sacrifice, it may be safer to come up with realistic boundaries for yourself and with a partner. We all have our weaknesses. It may be wise to make a list of your weaknesses and identify what you know to be green, yellow and red areas for yourself. Green of course means go, it is a comfortable and safe place that won't hinder your obedience to God. Red areas are situations you know you are subject to falling fast and hard. Be honest with yourself and with your partner. For some, holding hands denotes childhood affection and would be very much a green area. For another, holding hands is a deeply intimate act of affection which can be a trigger to being led by the hand to the bedroom.

Is kissing before marriage a sin? No. However, there are various levels of kissing. A peck on the lips can quickly turn into a hot and heavy makeout session leading to deeper levels of intimacy if you aren't careful. For this reason, many celibate couples opt to reserve kissing for marriage as well. If you think of each act of intimacy as being connected to your worship, it should automatically set the spiritual barometer. There is always a war going on between the spirit and the flesh. The flesh longs to test the limits. To be an overcomer on this walk, you must help yourself as much as possible. It is a good idea to set your own personal boundaries. Even with setting boundaries, it is all an act of will and choice. If you will yourself to give in and have sex, no pre-determined boundary can stop you. Likewise, if you resolve to be obedient, you can lie beside someone naked and not have sex. Do I recommend you testing your will power to this degree? No. However, it is factual that some people have greater thresholds for self-control than others.

Let's consider nighttime dating as the yellow zone. There is absolutely nothing wrong with going to dinner and a movie after the sunset. But I must caution you, most people are more prone to combine a glass of wine or a cocktail with dinner. Once again, know your limitations. Perhaps daytime dates are best during courtship with your future husband or wife.

I remember one of the first real dates someone took me on in college, was out to a fancy steakhouse. He ordered me my first martini and boy was it sweet and smooth. One minute we were laughing and joking and the next I had to rush to the restroom. After that one drink, I was stumbling to properly wipe myself. I indulged in one more drink because after you loosen up from the first one, it's only natural to say YES to the second. Before I knew it we were in a cab headed to his run down city apartment. Did we have sex? No, but there was a heavy make out session on his couch and I felt very uncomfortable spending the night. Introducing alcohol will bring down your inhibitions and makes it very easy to throw your self-control out of the window. Many dates have turned into heated make out sessions as a result of late night dating and one or two drinks. It doesn't take a rocket scientist to see how heavy kissing and fondling quickly puts you in the red zone. For some of you who have challenges determining what types of activities are safe or not, first, determine your threshold to physical intimacy.

Disclaimer: For all you spiritual police out there, this book is for the average person who wants to engage in dating while maintaining celibacy.

Green: Holding hands, kiss on the cheek, short hugs, dates during the day and going your separate ways after.

Yellow: Longer extended kisses, touching body parts through clothing, touching/grabbing/ rubbing.

1. "I'm very new to celibacy": Stay in the green zone until you have practiced going home after dates instead of back to the other person's place. Practice establishing boundaries and breaking habitual behavior patterns that have led you to the bedroom.

2. "I've been celibate a little while but I realize I still need boundaries": You might be safe in the yellow, but be careful.

3. "I have been celibate for several years and am able to withstand close intimacy and affection without giving in": Yellow shouldn't be too difficult, unless each year is becoming harder and harder vs. easier.

Red: Body massage without clothing, sleepovers, hanging out in the house at night, any contact with private parts with or without clothing, phone sex, hot tubs at night, siting in a car together at night for too long, showers together, extended kisses, touching body parts through clothing, kissing on trigger zones, or dry humping any private part through clothing. Red should be off limits to everyone practicing celibacy, regardless of how strong-willed you are.

It's always best not to play with fire. Some of the yellow and red areas will leave at least one person thinking "Well, we've gone this far, we might as well go all the way". It is never too late to say NO, but it's wiser to stay away from the catalysts that create a fire than to have to stop a fire once it's been ignited. Establishing boundaries may require a little trial and error, but anyone who has been successful at living a celibate lifestyle is aware of his/her weaknesses and learns to steer clear of situations that trigger them.

Just as it is possible to have sex devoid of intimacy, it is likewise possible to be intimate without having sex. Allow God to be your primary consultant. Ask Him to lead, guide and direct you in determining which boundaries are required for you to please Him and remain celibate. We want to steer clear of having a form of godliness, but denying its power.

God desires to be included in everything we do. He is a trusted friend like no other, standing by to intercede on your behalf, work through you and speak to you. Physical intimacy is a way of expressing your affection towards another. Tread lightly and carefully. See how you are able to maintain obedience first in the green before testing the yellow waters.

The initial stages of dating should consist of a courtship of the man maknig his interntions clear to the woman. Spend the first few weeks and even months getting to know the person. Gain a clear understanding of what each person's intentions are from the onset of dating. If they say they aren't looking for commitment, believe them! Know that this person could be a potential friend with benefits and this type of arrangement would've been perfect in the past. During this season of your life, you are not looking for a friend with benefits. Be clear, you are seeking God for your potential lifelong mate. What once may have been ideal may now be a situation you need to walk away from quickly.

Physical intimacy can wait. You have your whole life to express your sexuality in marriage. Re-gain control of your loins. Believe it or not, sex in a relationship can put up invisible blinders between you and your partner. Sex replaces good communication. Before marriage, it is vital to cultivate building blocks of solid, unmasked communication. Mutually satisfying sex will cause even the best of us to ignore and turn a blind eye to critical issues that need to be resolved for the sake of not losing the pleasure. This is a trap.

Flee from sexual immorality. All other sins a person commits are outside the body, but whoever sins sexually, sins against their own body.
1Corinthians 6:18

I find it very compelling that out of all the sins one can commit, sexual immorality is the only one, which a person can commit against his/her own body. The Bible is implying not only are you grieving the Holy Spirit, but you are hurting and sinning against yourself. By feeding your flesh and satisfying your body you are in fact, violating yourself and God's temple. To recognize when you are in violation of God and yourself, you must first value God's feelings towards you and value yourself worth and your soul. Are the temporary moments of pleasure worth sinning against your own body?

Victory

I hope you now see that success in celibacy empowers you to fully become who God called you to be and to value yourself through the eyes of God. I am merely a vessel who ventured to obey God. After completing graduate school, my life took an unexpected turn. I received the unmistakable call from God to share and preach the gospel of love and salvation. I was well-ordered by God to rest from the pursuit of my career and enter the ministry.

I was led by a fellow Evangelist to a Baptist church that affirmed my call and allowed me to serve as the pastor's assistant. Now operating in the surrendered place of servitude in the church, I was quickly elevated to the Minister over Prayer and Theater Arts and later ordained a reverend.

While none of this made sense in my carnal mind, my spirit knew God had been calling me closer and closer to Him for ministering to others. Like God instructing Samson not to cut his hair, I was commanded to see the celibate journey all the way through to completion. Words cannot articulate the enormity of the weight of this conviction at this point in my life. I knew I was on the path and there was no turning back. For two years, my days were spent riding my bike to a small church near the beach where I worked in a tiny, hot office often frustrated by non-operable printers and office machines. There was no glitz, glamour or self-glory. While humbled by the call of God on my life, I was depressed that my career was not going in the direction I'd previously envisioned. Yet, I focused on my purpose and remained steadfast in the Lord. When you take on the vow of becoming celibate by surrendering your entire being to God, He will entrust you with more opportunities to surrender.

During this season, I'd entertain the occasional date, but I was committed to the vow I'd made to God. I knew my worth. No man could sweet talk me out of my integrity and commitment to obedience. I knew God had a chosen mate for me. I knew I was worthy of love and was unwilling to trade a moment of passion for my purpose. Contrary to the world's advice to "put myself out there", my job was to stay hidden in Christ, while abounding in the works of the Lord. The Season of Stillness prepared me for the season of waiting to be found.

One day, while working in the church office, I received an email from a former classmate (I vaguely remembered) from Howard University who had just made the cross-country trek from NY to LA. He was reaching out to everyone he knew from college, now living in LA. He extended the invitation to meet up for dinner and drinks. Since real dates were few and far between, I happily conceded to meeting up with him and re-connecting.

Our initial call to set up our date was spent talking about God. He was transparent about his spiritual walk and having been led by God to move to LA. I committed our initial meet-up to prayer and even took a girlfriend along to be a buffer. It had been years since I'd seen this guy. He could've been crazy for all I knew. Something in my spirit felt like God was OK with this date. I encourage you to commit all of your dates to prayer and ask God to give you discernment about who is worthy of your priceless time and attention.

When we met up, it was like time stood still. He looked refined, handsome, patient and accomplished. We locked eyes from across the room and something deep inside knew He was my husband. Yet, I didn't turn all psycho and begin planning our wedding in my head. I quietly acknowledged the revelation of the Holy Spirit, continued to pray for confirmation and allowed him to properly court me.

Our first date was quite refreshing. He, unlike most men in LA, was genuinely interested in me (the person). I was comfortable candidly talking to him about my journey in life. He was impressed by my accomplishments and humored by my daily bike rides to the church. More importantly, we were equally yoked in his hunger to seek the Lord for all things. In past relationships, the one thing often missing was a mutual hunger to genuinely live for God.

Our lives drew great parallels and complemented each other perfectly. We both grew up in the Baptist church but could relate to the suffering of straying away and living life on our own accord. God had been calling us both back into relationship with Him for a purpose beyond our greatest expectation or desire.

I had been successfully celibate during my "Season of Stillness" two years prior to him entering my life. After a few dates, I made my intentions clear. At this point, too much was on the line to give in. While, the voice of the young man who once told me, "No grown man is going to wait for you to have sex until marriage" I knew if God was real, and if in fact he was my husband, we would wait for each other.

Sure enough, he did and we didn't rush. He courted me for quite some time and we dated, getting to know each other inside and out for three and a half years before he proposed. God showed us the heart of one another and allowed us to walk through many ups and downs including seasons of lack and grief during our courtship. Through it all, we knew God had a purpose for our lives and we were committed to walking together in obedience. He believed in the vision God had given me for Ministry and the Arts and became my greatest advocate and support in fulfilling God's assignments in my life. While being celibate as a man comes with an entirely different stigma and nature of temptation, not once did he try to entice me to compromise. He too, was tired of living beneath God's standard. We built a foundation of love and trust based on our common goal to create a legacy of faith and prosperity for the generations to come.

I will forever be in awe of seeing God's promises come to pass. I'm a living witness that God's promises are 100% true and will be fulfilled in the lives of those who dare to have blind faith out of a love for Him. The Holy Spirit had broken the chains of desperation, sexual addiction and fornication. He empowered us to complete our celibate journey, together.

After years of seeking love in all the wrong places and compromising my initial conviction to wait until marriage, God wiped my slate clean. Even when I failed, He never relented in expressing His all-consuming love for me. All along, he was preparing me to receive His best. He was preparing my husband (a man after his own heart) behind the scenes. He brought my husband to me literally and figuratively. I didn't have to join a dating website or "put myself out there" to attract suitors. God doesn't need us to orchestrate His plans. He needs us to surrender to His will for our lives.

Six years of celibacy weren't easy, but with each year it became easier. God is so faithful and is a rewarder of those who diligently seek Him. He blessed us with a beautiful, intimate, fairytale wedding in California where our friends and family traveled far and wide to witness our union. Three years later, God filled and opened a place in my heart I never knew existed when he chose me to give birth to a beautiful baby girl, Lulu Saint-Claire. He allowed me to feel the tremendous honor of becoming a mother. God fulfilled the promises which He revealed to me in my lowest moments and He will do the same for you!

Children are a heritage from the Lord, offspring a reward from Him.
Psalm 127:3

Hold your horses! I'm not promising you that if you make the decision to wait you'll get everything you want in the timing you envisioned. However, standing on the promises of God, I guarantee that by making the commitment to obey God, He will shower you with custom-made blessings according to His will for your life. Starting today, get out of your own way and surrender to the unique plans He has for you. Exchange the world's way for the perfect will of God. Our Lord and Savior is able to do exceedingly above all you can think or imagine. I'm a living witness that God will lift you up when you are weak, deliver you from the bondage of fornication and carry you down the path of peace and righteousness for His name sake. He is worthy of your love, trust and total surrender. Commit to God this area of your life, and you too will be successful in celibacy!

If they obey and serve him, they will spend the rest of their days in prosperity and their years in contentment.
Job 36:11

ABOUT THE AUTHOR

Shea was born in Richmond, VA and raised in a loving, Christian household as daughter to John and Jewel Scott. As a teenager, Shea was a panelist on the BET show, Teen Summit. She graduated with a Bachelor of Fine Arts degree from Howard University where she became a member of DIVA, Inc. and earned a Master of Fine Arts from UCLA. She also matriculated at Oxford University sharpening her skills as a classically trained actress. Shea answered the call to ministry after her tenure at UCLA and was ordained a minister and reverend at the First Baptist Church of Venice.

Shea Edwards is the co-founder of "Faith Rocks", an online Ministry, Blog and Talk Show dedicated to encouraging the world to incorporate faith into all aspects of life and provide practical tools to promoting prayer and a closer relationship with Jesus Christ. She and her husband began "Faith Rocks" in their studio apartment in Hollywood, CA. They also have a production company called "Cattle on a Hill". She was married to her husband Brandon in 2013 in Costa Mesa, CA. In 2016, Shea gave birth to their daughter, Lulu Saint-Claire and they currently reside in Inglewood, CA.

She is now on a global mission to help heal and empower the masses, particularly women, innovators, entrepreneurs and artists through the power of Christ. Shea is a free-spirited, artistic vessel living an intentional life of transparency to glorify God through her trials and triumphs. In her free time, she enjoys praying, online window shopping, swimming, laughing, catching up with friends over brunch, spending time in nature and traveling with her family.

Made in the USA
Middletown, DE
06 January 2023

21499587R00057